DATE DUE

JUN 17 91			
FEB 1 0 1992			
JUL 1 4 1993			
APR 2 1 1995			
OC 17 '97			

LETTERING

John Lancaster

Consultant: Henry Pluckrose

Photography: Chris Fairclough

FRANKLIN WATTS
London/New York/Sydney/Toronto

Copyright © 1988
Franklin Watts

Franklin Watts Inc
387 Park Avenue South
New York, NY 10016

ISBN: 0-531-10624-1

Library of Congress
Calalog Card
No: 88-50195

Design: Edward Kinsey

Editor: Jenny Wood

Printed in Belgium

DEDICATION
This book is dedicated to you, the young inspiring calligrapher who is prepared to learn how to write a formal script. You must stick at it. At times you will find the going hard. Tell yourself you are going to succeed. You will, I trust, become a much better calligrapher than I am and I also hope you will go on to do some interesting work. Always be prepared to help others – some of whom may be much younger than you are – and try to inspire them with confidence. It is up to you to persevere so that you can help to carry on the skilful traditions of a beautiful art form and help it to be preserved and to flourish in the future.
John Lancaster

Contents

Equipment and materials

Brushes (squirrel/sable-type, Nos 4 or 5)

Drawing or writing board, about 30cm × 40cm (12″ ×16″) (either a strong piece of card, or a piece of hardboard such as Masonite)

Drawing pins (or mapping pins)

Eraser (soft rubber)

Inks (black and colored fountain pen inks)

Jam jars (old) in which to stand pens

Masking tape

Paper – white typing paper
– white cartridge or drawing paper
(later you may wish to buy some hand-made paper or parchment)

Paper clips

Pencil (H or 2H)

Pens (felt-tipped calligraphy markers, dip pens, or calligraphy fountain pens

Ruler (30.5cm (12″), plastic or wooden)

Saucers or dishes (old) (or paper plates)

Scissors

Scrap material – e.g. pieces of cardboard, pieces of wood, newspapers, paper towel, matchsticks, cocktail sticks, pieces of wire

Shoe box (or similar container) in which to store your pens, inks, ruler, pencils etc.

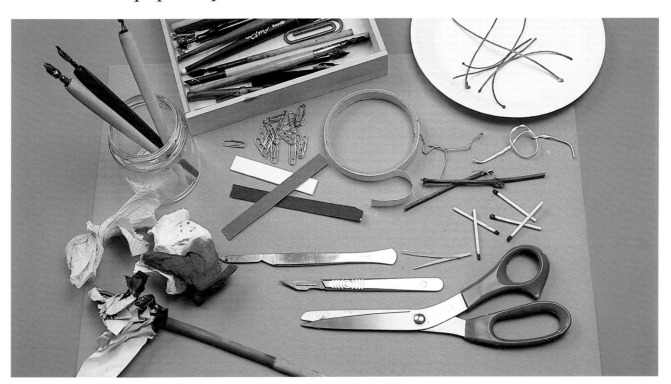

Getting ready

What is calligraphy?

The simplest answer to this question is that calligraphy is skillful mark-making done with a pen. It is, in effect, a carefully controlled form of drawing. It is the art of fine penmanship which, in the Medieval period, led to the production of lovely manuscript books. These were written and illuminated by scribes in monasteries and abbeys.

This book will introduce you to the materials and basic skills you need to master the art of penmanship. It has been written to encourage you to experiment quite freely with marks on paper, and the suggestions given on the following pages should help you to use materials and writing tools in an interesting way. Some guidance is given about simple layout and design, but you will be asked to be inventive so that you can develop confidence and skill.

You will be shown how to construct letters that are open or round in character. This is known as "round-hand" lettering.

Some hints

If possible, work in a quiet place where you can concentrate.

Cover your work-top (table, desk, etc) with an old blanket, a sheet of plastic or some old newspaper.

Cover yourself too. Overalls, a smock or an old shirt will do nicely.

1 Pens must have square ends. Use fountain pen inks in a variety of colors.

Have ready your basic kit of materials and equipment (see page 4).

Pens

Your pen must be a "chisel" or "edged" pen – in other words, it must have a *square end* (see picture **2**). The reason for this is that the kind of calligraphy you will learn in this book is dependent upon thick and thin strokes. These are produced by a pen with a square writing edge.

Felt-tipped markers are excellent for beginners, and are recommended for use with the activities in this book. You can buy them in some stationery stores or from art supply stores. Choose 3.5mm and 5.0mm marker pens. A few of the many makes of felt-tipped markers are:
– Speedball Elegant Writer Calligraphy Marker pens
– Eberhard Faber Design Calligraphy Art Pens
– Crayola Creative Lettering Kit

2 A square writing edge is needed to produce thick and thin strokes.

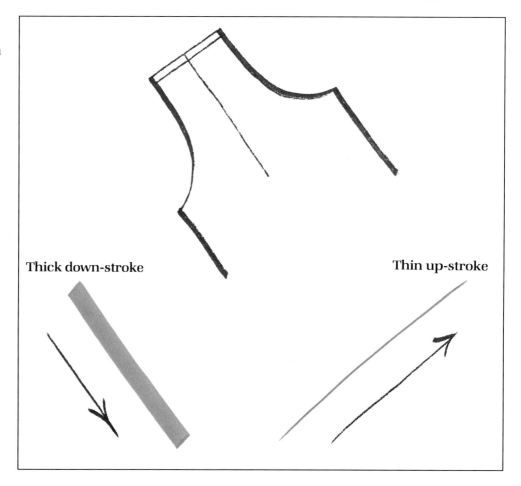

Thick down-stroke

Thin up-stroke

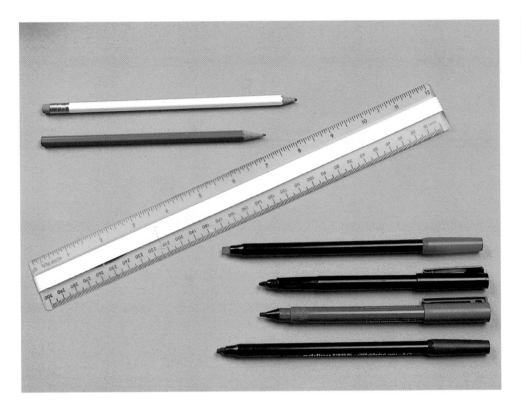

3 Felt-tipped marker pens are excellent for beginners.

– Niji Calligraphy Marker Pens

Dip pens (so-called because they are dipped into ink) consist of penholders (plastic or wood), metal nibs (William Mitchell Rexel Round Hand Nos 1, 2 & 3 steel nibs are excellent) and brass reservoirs which are attached underneath the nibs to hold small quantities of ink. (William Mitchell Slippon brass reservoirs are designed to be used with the Round Hand nibs.) Practice with a No 1½ or a No 2. Coit and Speedball pens are also good for this purpose.

Use dip pens after you have become proficient with felt tipped pens.

Calligraphy fountain pens are made by Osmiroid, Koh-I-Noor, and Platignum. They are nice to use because they are designed to hold ink in cartridge form. However, their nibs are not as fine as dip pens.

Toward the end of the book you will be shown how to make a quill pen from a feather.

4 An example of a
William Mitchell Rexel
Round Hand pen nib.

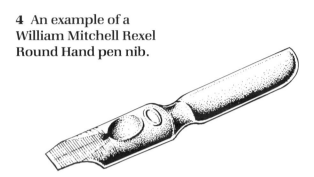

5 Quill and reed pens.

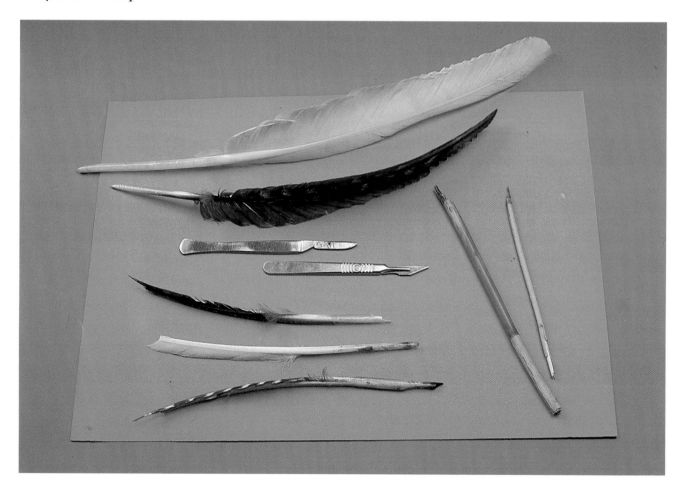

Experimental mark making

Artists have always experimented, for that is the best way to make new discoveries. Primitive people drew simple images of people and animals on cave walls many centuries ago. These simple images are known as pictograms and were the beginnings from which ideograms and then stylized letter images grew. (An ideogram is a simple drawing which expresses an idea.)

Try making your own experimental marks. You will need paper, pens, inks, an old saucer or plate for each ink color, newspaper, cardboard, scrap materials (e.g. twig, bamboo, matchstick, piece of wire), and scissors. You can even use your fingertips to make images. Be inventive and bold in what you do.

1 Two pictograms, of a horse and a man.

2 Two ideograms – the first, a drawing of an eye with a tear indicating weeping or crying; the second, a modern ideogram of a crossed-out iron. What do you think this crossed-out iron means?

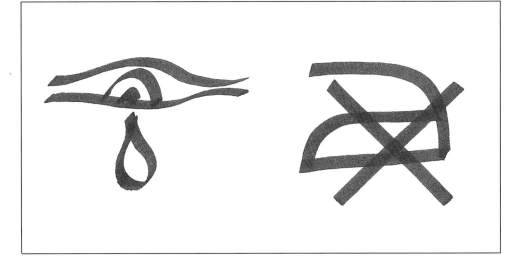

3 (Right) Put a small quantity of ink on a saucer. Remember to put the top back on the bottle. Dip a piece of screwed-up newspaper into the ink. Now make some strong marks on your paper. Use straight lines, curved lines, dots and spots, circles, and any other images you like.

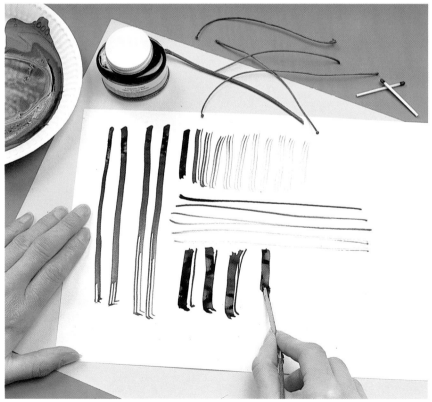

4 Repeat some of these experiments, using a twig, a matchstick or a piece of bamboo or reed.

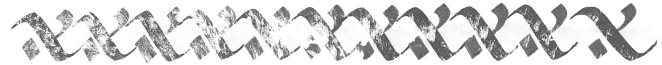
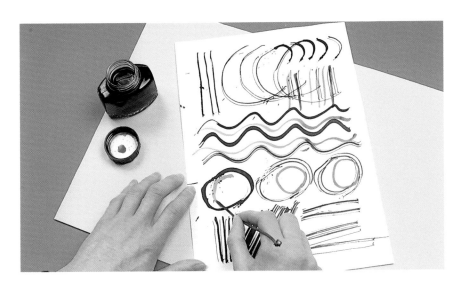

5 You can make finer lines and dots as well as more delicate shapes with a piece of wire dipped into ink.

6 (Right) Take a piece of cardboard (approximately 1cm (⅜″) wide) and cut it straight across the end so that it is like a square-edged pen. Dip it into the ink.

7 Use this simple "cardboard" pen to draw some strong, firm images. (Do not attempt any letters yet.) Go on to do some zig-zag lines and curved shapes. If the cardboard becomes soggy, simply cut a new straight chisel end.

In order to move on to the making of letters you will find it helpful to do simple "dot-and-stick" letters. These are made up of straight lines, curved lines and dots.

Words can be made to look much more exciting if black or colored lines are drawn round them.

1 The blue dot-and-stick letters were done with a felt-tipped calligraphy marker. The black ones and the outlines were drawn with an ordinary black ballpoint.

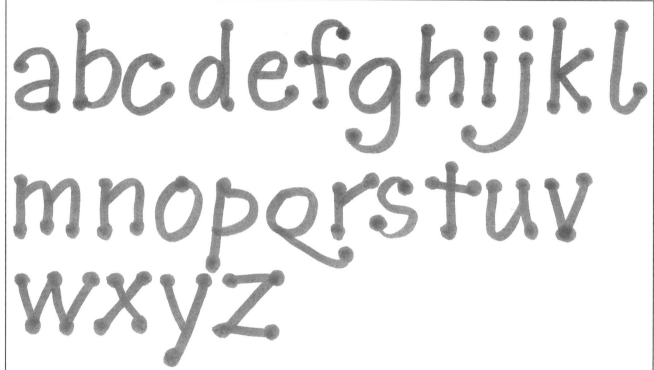

Making a start with calligraphy

A comfortable writing position is very important. You will need a drawing or writing board. This should have a wide piece of paper or cardboard taped to it so that the paper on which you write can be slipped underneath. The wide piece of paper or cardboard will act as a protection and can also be used for trying out your pens.

1 Sit at a table with your writing board resting in your lap at an angle of about 40°– 45°. Never attempt to write flat on a table top.

2 The best placement for your writing is just above the top edge of the protective paper or card. To determine this writing position, and therefore where the protective shield should go, take a pen in your right hand then place the writing edge on the angled board.

3 (Above) Most calligraphers are right-handed and, as shown here, should hold the pen so that if points roughly over the right shoulder.

4 (Right) The square edge of the pen should be held at an angle of 30° to the horizontal writing line. This angle should not vary. The pen's square edge and the constant angle give the letters their strong character.

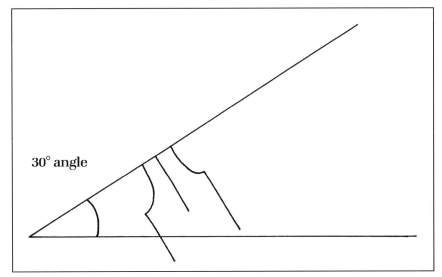

30° angle

Pen patterns

Every calligrapher likes to practice, particularly before beginning an important piece of work. Pen patterns are used to develop skill, rhythm and evenness. Remember – practice makes perfect!

1 Take one of your pens and do a series of straight vertical lines, evenly spaced, each about 2cm (1″) in length.

2 (Left) Repeat this process but this time do horizontal, sloping, curved and zig-zag lines.

3 (Opposite page) Now simply have fun doing pen patterns of all kinds.

Guidelines will ensure that your lines of lettering are well spaced and straight.

A special guide sheet has been prepared to assist you (see page 19).

This guide sheet has been drawn up for size 5.0mm pens, so for your first attempts at writing, use a 5.0mm felt-tipped pen, or a Rexel or other 5.0m calligraphy pen.

1 Place a sheet of paper over the guide sheet, and hold it in position with two paper clips on the top edge. The guidelines will now show through from underneath. These will help you with your first attempt at writing.

2 The size of a letter is determined by the width of your pen's square writing edge. Capital letters, for instance, are seven pen widths high from the writing line. The body of a lower-case ("small") letter is four pen widths high.

3 (Opposite page) GUIDE SHEET The writing lines are drawn a little heavier than the rest and go right to the edges of the sheet to make them more distinctive.

Writing line

Writing line

Side margin

Writing line

Side margin

Writing line

Writing line

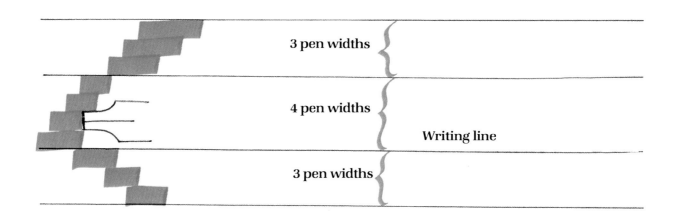

3 pen widths

4 pen widths

Writing line

3 pen widths

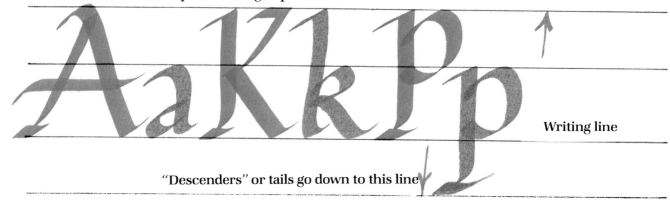

"Ascenders" and capital letters go up to this line

Writing line

"Descenders" or tails go down to this line

4 If a lower-case letter has an "ascender" (the top part of a letter such as b, d or k), the ascender goes up seven pen widths from the writing line. If a lower-case letter has a "descender" (the part that hangs below the line in letters such as g, j, p, q and y), it goes down three pen widths from the writing line.

Two important letters

The letter "I" is straight, and the letter "O" consists of curved strokes. As all the other letters of the alphabet result from either straight or curved strokes, you will find them easier to do if you first learn to write "I" and "O."

When writing round-hand letters, you must follow a set sequence of strokes. These are shown in the pictures. The arrows indicate the direction of each stroke.

The capital letter "I"

1 Take your pen and make a fine line, called a "serif" (1). Move the pen down, vertically, from the top of the serif without lifting it from the paper (2). This will give you a strong, upright stroke. Add a small, straight stroke across the bottom of the vertical stroke (3). This is the foot on which the letter 'I' stands.

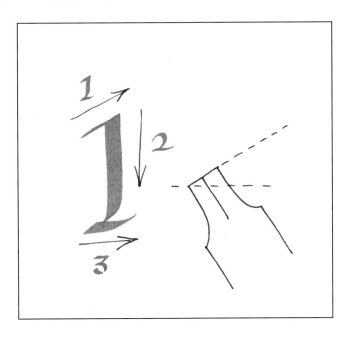

The lower-case "i"

2 Make a serif so that the top of it just meets the guideline for the top of the lower-case letters (1). Without lifting your pen, move it down vertically and round it to the right at the bottom (2). This should be a continuous movement. To "dot" the letter "i" simply add a thin line above it (3).

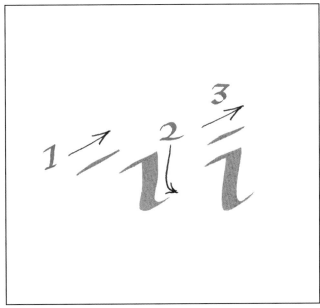

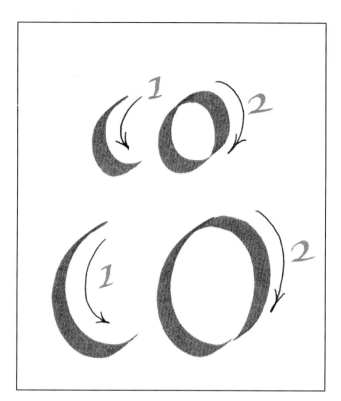

The letter 'O' (capital and lower-case)

3 With a smooth, unhurried movement of the pen, make the curved stroke on the left (1). Complete the letter by making a curved stroke on the right (2).

4 Practise writing both capital and lower-case 'I's and 'O's.

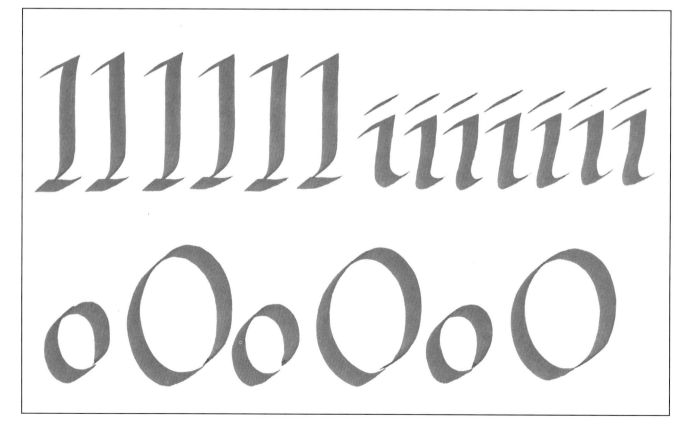

A serif can be a fine line or a kind of hook. It is used at the start of many letters. A true serif consists of three basic strokes.

5 (Left) The first stroke is a small hook.

6 (Right) Stroke 2 is a thin hairline.

7 (Left) The last stroke is the start of the main stroke (or a part of one of the following letters: b, d, h, i, j, k, l, p, u).

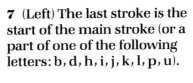

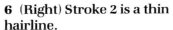

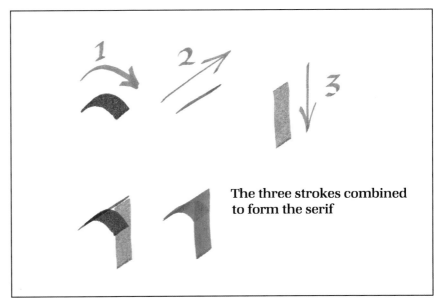

The three strokes combined to form the serif

8 Practise writing serifs.

You will be shown, step by step, how to construct the letters A and B. This will give you the correct procedure and then it is up to you to construct the remaining letters of the alphabet yourself.

A special circle guide has been drawn up for you to use when writing letters. It is designed for a 5.0mm felt-tipped calligraphy marker. Place it underneath a sheet of paper. The circles and lines will show through.

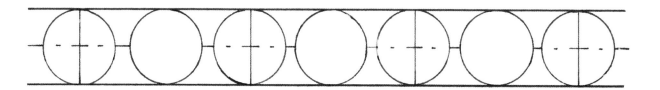

Lower-case letter guide

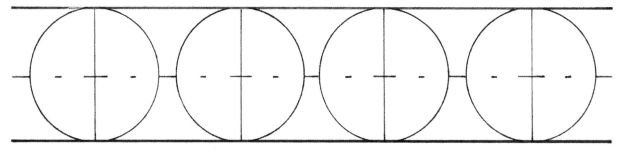

Capital letter guide

1 Follow the lines on the circle guide when writing letters.

2 (Right) First make the left-hand stroke of the capital letter "A" (1). Add the foot (2), then the right-hand sloping stroke (3). Finally, add the cross stroke (4). This should be parallel with the horizontal writing guideline.

3 (Left) The finished capital letter "A".

4 (Below) Make the serif and vertical stroke of the letter "B" in two smooth, unhurried movements (1 and 2). Now make the top, curved stroke (3). Add the lower, curved stroke (4). Complete the letter (5).

5 The finished capital letter "B".

6 This alphabet of capital letters was written on paper placed over the circle guide. Before writing your own alphabet freehand in the same way, place a sheet of paper over this alphabet and trace the letters. This will help you learn how to do the different shapes. The numbers tell you in what order to do the strokes. The arrows show you in which direction to move your pen.

These follow a pattern
similar to that of the
capital letters.

1 (Right) Do stroke 1 of the
letter "a." Add stroke 2.

2 (Below) Do strokes 1 and 2 of
the letter "b." Add stroke 3.

3 (Right) Before writing your
own lower-case alphabet
freehand, place a sheet of
paper over this alphabet and
trace the letters. This will help
you learn how to do the
different shapes. The numbers
tell you in what order to do the
strokes. The arrows show you
in which direction to move
your pen.

4 These two alphabets were written freehand without the use of guidelines. When you feel confident enough, try your own freehand alphabets.

ABCDEF
GHIJKLM
NOPQRSTU
VWX YZ

abcdefghijklm
nopqrstuvwx
yz

The most important thing about lines of continuous writing is that they should be easy to read.

1 Keep all the spaces between the letters the same size. They should appear even, and should balance each other. You will need to use your eyes to judge these spaces, as you cannot measure them.

Lines of scri

lines of script should be evenly spaced

Space

2 The spaces between the words should be the size of a letter "o".

SPACESOFEQU

ALOTOOAOLETTER

Space

"O" approximately

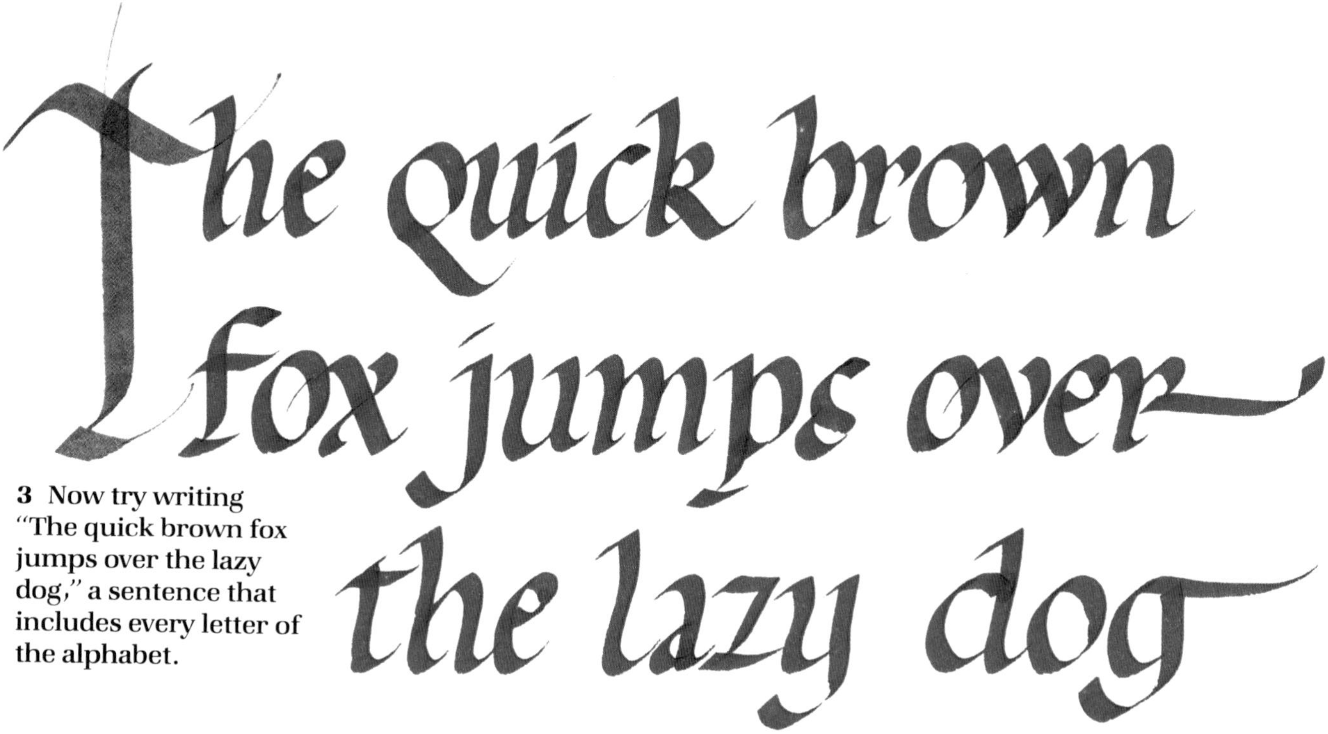

The quick brown fox jumps over the lazy dog

3 Now try writing "The quick brown fox jumps over the lazy dog," a sentence that includes every letter of the alphabet.

Numerals (numbers) are written the way you write letters. Remember to hold the pen at a constant angle of about 30°.

1 The numbers tell you in what order to do the strokes. The arrows show you in which direction to move your pen.

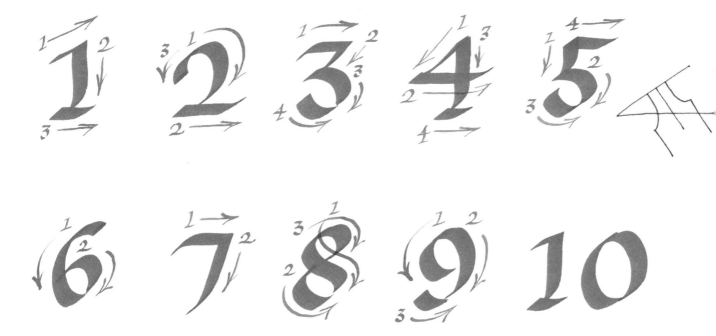

Broadsheets

A broadsheet is a piece of design work or calligraphy contained, like a picture, on a single sheet of paper. Posters, notices, and single sheets of prose or poetry are examples of broadsheets. Special work can be framed.

Every broadsheet is different in content, size and arrangement of wording and/or decoration. When you set about planning such a piece of work, you need to start by drawing marginal lines lightly with a pencil.

You can keep your paper vertical, to give you a "portrait" broadsheet, or you can turn it sideways, to make a "landscape" broadsheet.

1 Top and side margins should be the same. Margins at the bottom of the sheet should be wider. They can be 1½ or even 2 times the width of the top margin.

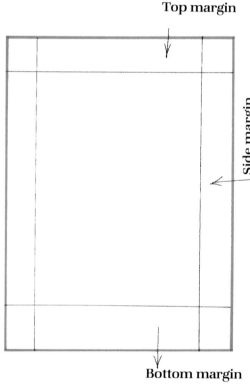

A "portrait" broadsheet

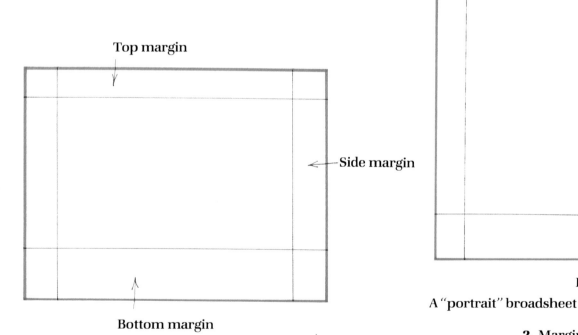

A "landscape" broadsheet

2 Margin sizes will vary with each piece of work. The suggestions given here are simply a guide for you to follow.

The actual wording on a notice, poster or poem can be written starting from the left-hand margin. As the lengths of the lines will vary, this will produce an uneven margin on the right-hand side of the sheet. Sometimes this can be quite effective.

Alternatively, the lines of lettering can be centered.

3 To center lettering, draw a faint pencil line vertically through the middle of the sheet. Then, on a practice sheet, write each line of lettering. Measure each line and find its center. Mark these centers in pencil on your broadsheet, and complete the lettering.

Center line

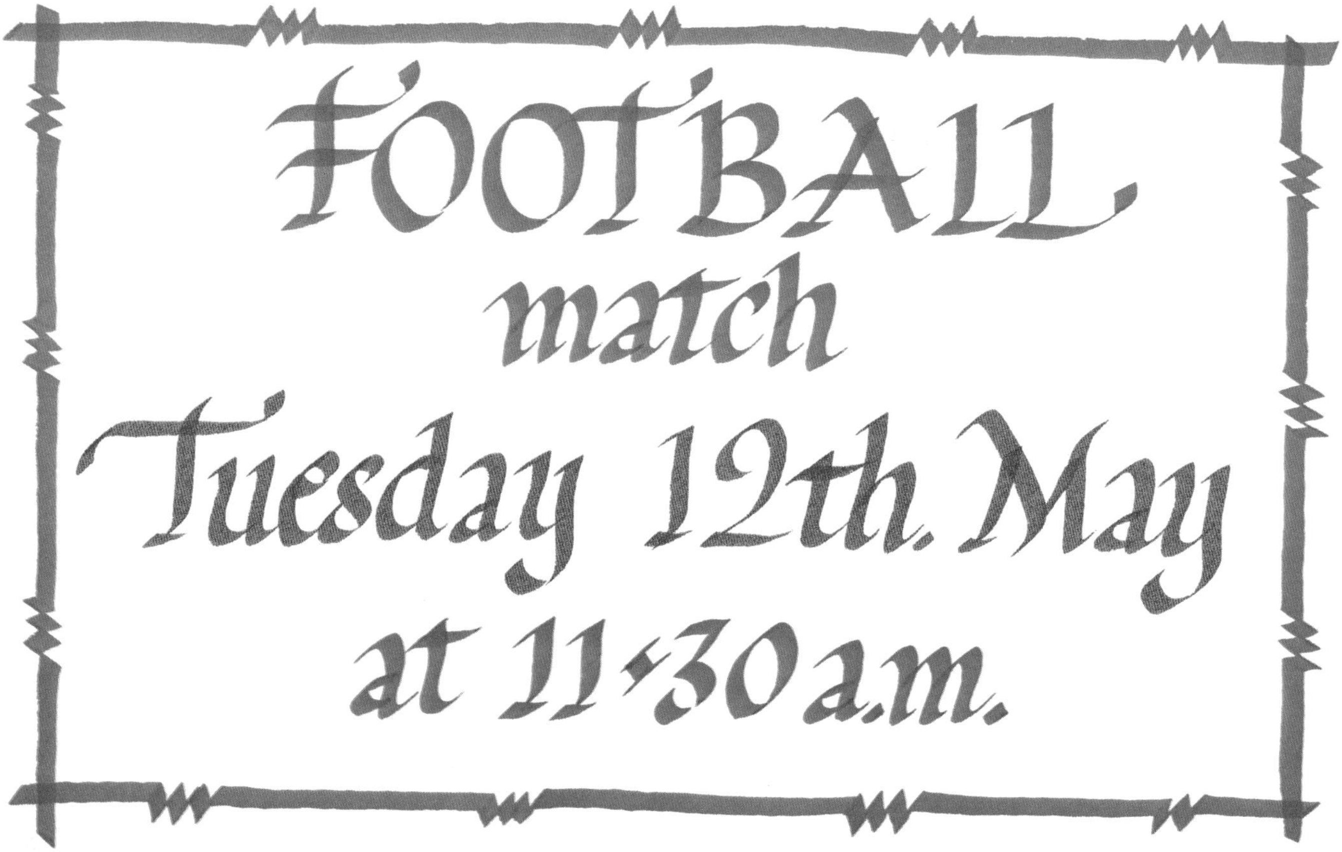

FOOTBALL
match
Tuesday 12th. May
at 11·30 a.m.

4 An example of a finished landscape broadsheet with centered lettering.

If you use two or more different sizes of pen you will be able to emphasize important parts of your design. This will add variety to your broadsheet. The addition of a colored title can be most attractive.

Sometimes the first letter of each line can be written in color and the remainder in black.

A book in calligraphy is made up of a number of "page-openings." These are folded, and slipped one inside the other. They are finished off by being bound together.

You could design a page-opening like the one here.

1 The proportions of the margins on a page-opening should be approximately: top margin = 2; bottom margin = 4; side margins = 3; center margins = 3 (divided into two smaller margins of 1½). Your writing and illustrations will fit into the large rectangular areas on the pages.

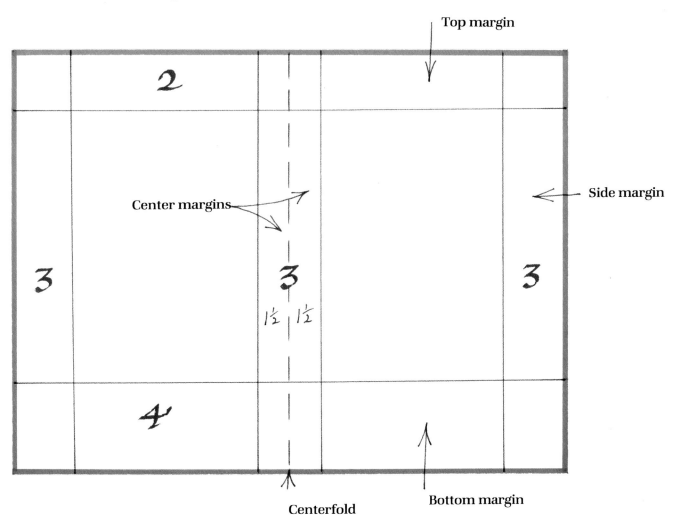

Top margin

Center margins

Side margin

2

3   3   3

1½ | 1½

4

Centerfold

Bottom margin

Inventive calligraphy

Once you have mastered round-hand letters you will find that using a calligraphy pen can be fun. It will enable you to invent freely.

You need not stick to writing words, poems or set texts. You can be really creative.

Here are a few starting points and ideas.

1 Make a dot in the middle of a sheet of paper. Now write six capital letter "A"s in a line to the right of the dot.

2 Turn the paper upside down. Now write six capital letter "R"s in a line to the right of the dot.

3 Turn the paper half-way around, and write another letter five times in a diagonal line. Vary the sizes of your lines of letters, and use pens of different colors.

4 Turn the paper around again, and write another diagonal line, this time of seven letters.

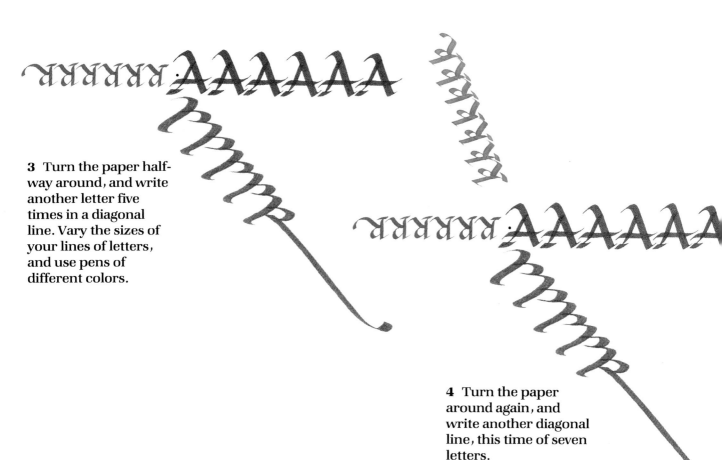

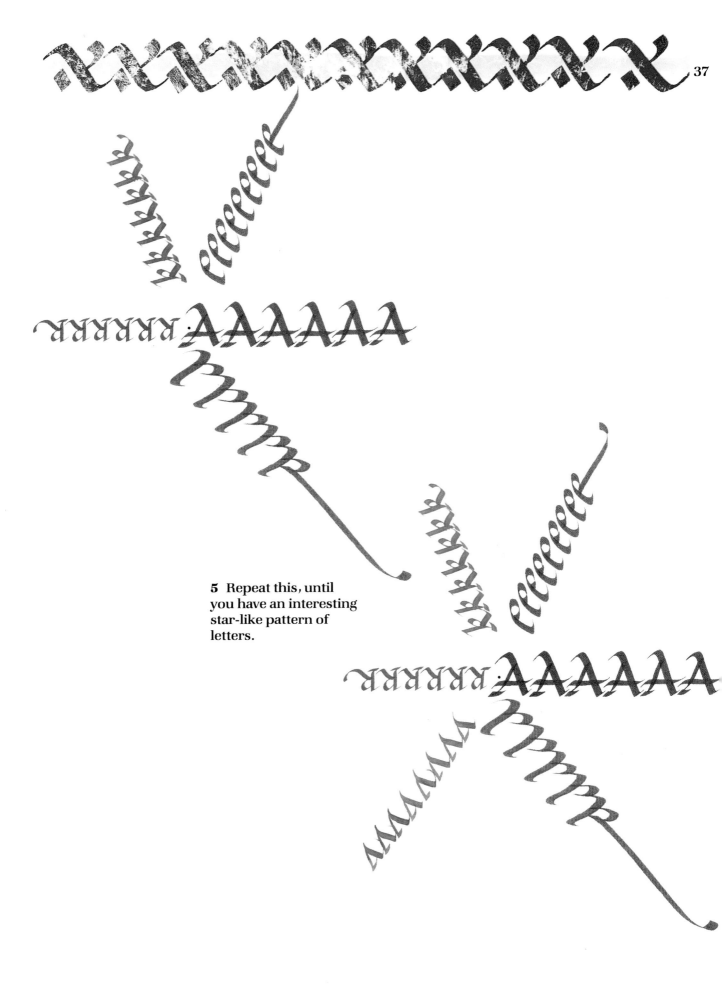

5 Repeat this, until you have an interesting star-like pattern of letters.

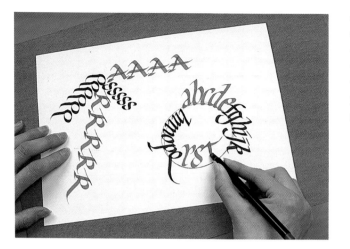

6 Place a saucer on a sheet of paper and draw round it with a pencil. With a felt-tipped calligraphy pen write an alphabet of lower-case letters around the pencil circle. You will have to turn the paper as you work, to enable you to write correctly.

7 (Below) This piece of work is based on a triangle. It was done in three stages. First, a triangle was drawn to form the basis of the design.

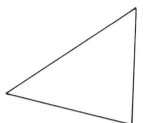

8 A lower-case alphabet was written around the edges of the triangle and some letters were placed inside.

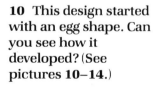

9 Some of the spaces inside and between the letters were filled in with a ballpoint pen.

10 This design started with an egg shape. Can you see how it developed? (See pictures **10–14**.)

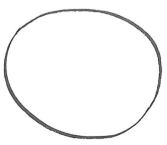

11

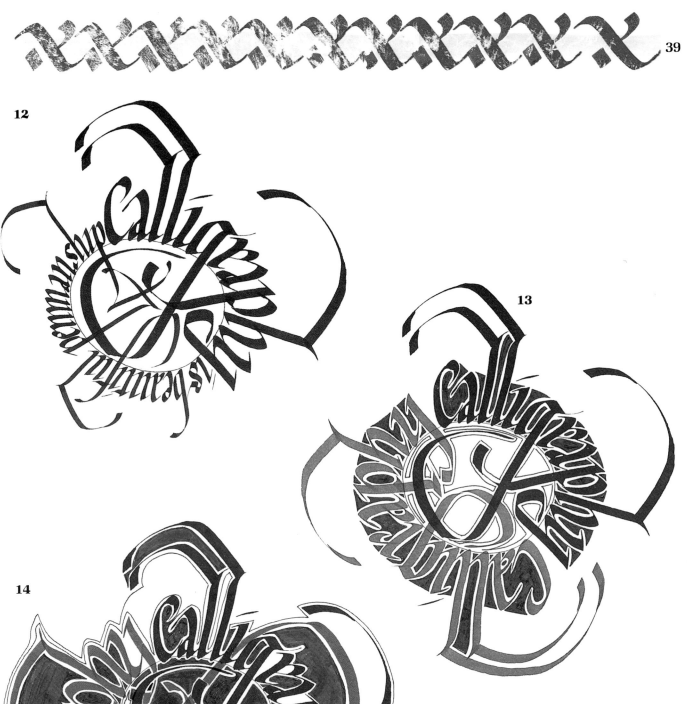

12

13

14

Here are some examples of
inventive calligraphy.

These examples of calligraphy show it being used purposefully. Each one has been carefully designed and the lettering is clear and easy to read.

20 A luncheon menu written with a pen and then printed.

21 A title for a small brochure.

22 A notice for a classroom door.

23 A Christmas card design.

Making a quill pen

A pen cut from a feather is called a quill. The most suitable feathers are what are called "flight feathers." These come from the leading part of a bird's wing and are strong and tough.

Calligraphers prefer the feathers of swans, geese and turkeys. Turkey feathers are the most commonly used, as goose feathers are difficult to obtain and swans are protected birds. If you cannot obtain a turkey feather, try cutting quill pens from the flight feathers of hens or crows. You may be able to find these on the ground.

Before you attempt to cut a quill, the feather must dry out well. This usually takes about eighteen months, which is a long time, but you can experiment with new or "green" feathers.

You will need a sharp knife or penknife to cut your quill, and a needle.

1 A selection of "flight feathers."

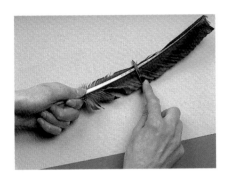

2 (Left) Hold the feather and cut it so that it is about 18cm or 20cm (7″ or 8″) long.

3 (Right) Strip off the barbs.

4 Hold the shortened feather in your left hand and place it upside down on a hard surface. Hold it firmly. Make a slightly curving cut away from you into the shaft of the feather. Start about 2cm (1″) from its tip. Cut toward the tip. Now make two further cuts – one to the right-hand and the other to the left-hand side of the shaft. These, too, should be slightly curved. They should give you two parallel lines which go to the tip.

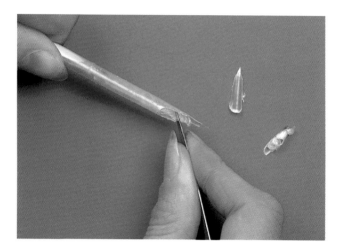

5 (Left) Remove what is called the "pith" from inside the shaft of the feather with a needle or the point of a compass.

6 (Right) Place the tip of the feather on a hard surface (a sheet of glass or formica will do) and cut a square end at an oblique angle.

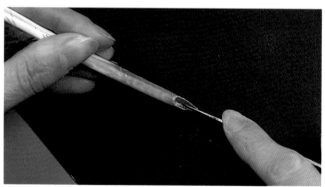

7 (Right) Turn the pen over and cut a slit near the tip. This will allow the ink to flow down to the writing edge.

8 (Left) Now try to write with your quill pen. Take a small brush full of ink and gently apply some to the rear part of the pen. Apply very little pressure on the paper – simply let the quill pen "flow" easily. (Do not dip the quill pen into ink, as that would make the ink flood on to your paper.)

A good quill pen makes a scratching noise. It will give you good thick strokes and delicate hairlines. When the tip becomes worn, simply cut a new tip.

Most of the materials mentioned in this book are easy to obtain. White typing paper can be bought at any stationery store – it is ideal for the kind of work you will be doing. Pens, inks, rulers, pencils etc can usually be found in local art-supply stores.

If you have difficulty obtaining exactly what you want, all of the following suppliers carry a selection of calligraphy materials.

Sax Arts & Crafts
P.O. Box 2002
Milwaukee, WI 53201
414-272-4900
1-800-242-4911

Dick Blick Art Materials
P.O. Box 1267
Galesburg, Il 61401
309-343-6181
1-800-447-8192

A.I. Friedman, Inc.
Art and Drafting Materials
25 W 45th Street
New York, NY 10036
212-575-0200

J.L. Hammett
P.O. Box 545
Braintree MA 02184

Triarco Arts & Crafts
14650 28th Ave. North
Plymouth, MN 55441
612-559-5590
800-328-3360

Some helpful books

Gourdie, Tom, *Calligraphy for the Beginner*, Taplinger Publishing Co., New York, 1979
Jarman, Christopher, *The Osmiroid Book of Calligraphy*, Osmiroid, Gosport, Hampshire, England, 1983
Shepherd, Margaret, *Learning Calligraphy*, Collier Books, division of MacMillan Publishing Co., New York, 1978
Baron, Nancy, *Getting Started in Calligraphy*, Sterling Publishing Co., New York, 1979
Ken Brown Books – a line sold by Hunt Manufacturing Co., Statesville, NC 28677:
The Ken Brown Calligraphy Handbook; and
The Ken Brown Calligraphy Resource Guide
There are also two videos: "Ken Brown's Old English Calligraphy" and "Ken Brown's Chancery Cursive Calligraphy"
Stoner, Charles, *Beautiful Italic Writing Made Easy*